Disclaimer

that results due to misinterpretation of guidelines and ideas presented in this Book.

Any views or opinions expressed here are strictly my own. While I am a writer who works for Citrix, I am not a Citrix writer; therefore, I am solely responsible for all content published here. This is a personal book, not a Citrix systems book.

Content published here is not read, reviewed, or approved in advance by Citrix and does not necessarily represent or reflect the views or opinions of Citrix or any of its divisions, subsidiaries, or business partners.

This eBook cannot be used as a substitute for professional advice.

At a Glance

FOR many years now, enterprises have pulled all the strings to revive desktop management. In the wake of the globalization of the workforce, ever-increasing corporate applications and increasing instances of security breaches, a technology was direly needed, one that not only addressed all of the issues that the IT landscape hurled its way, but one that accomplished this while keeping a tab on operational and capital costs. This is where Virtual Desktop Infrastructure, abbreviated as VDI, stepped into the picture.

VDI emerged as the new face of remote desktop management and met all expectations by breathing life into the idea of workforce mobility. Today, desktop virtualization is a synonym for organizational success that balances security, employee motivation and cost in one hand, and immense technical capability in the other.

This Book is an attempt at elucidating the unlimited potential of desktop virtualization and showing how easily it has transformed the business landscape. With the wealth of wisdom revealed in this Book, businesses will understand how VDI irons out all those wrinkles that stand between them and effective management of user environments.

In this Book, you will find answers to questions like:

- Which problems served as the bedrock for desktop virtualization?

- How did VDI emerge on the scene as the new face for desktop management?

- How can the use of VDI help businesses outshine and outpace others?

- What are the benefits that VDI rolled out with its inception?

- How does desktop virtualization take data security to new heights?

- What are some of the most useful VDI solutions available on the market?

- How did VDI help businesses get past conventional IT solutions?

- What are the different implementation scenarios that can work wonders for an organization?

Read on to find out how desktop virtualization turns simplified management of user desktops into a reality.

Contents

Introduction

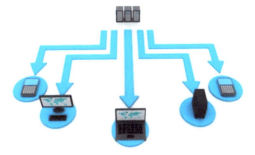

VIRTUAL Desktop Infrastructure reared its head on the II landscape as a new and unconventional means of managing user desktops. In layman's terms, VDI was introduced with the intent to separate a computer from the desktop environment.

VDI falls into a client-server model in which a 'virtualized' desktop is stored on a remote server and can be accessed whenever and wherever the user desires.

The technology resembles private cloud and SaaS (Software as a Service), and given the tremendous benefits it has to offer, more and more IT administrators are considering hosting and administering desktops on these virtual infrastructures, specifically in the datacenters.

The biggest advantage VDI has introduced is the fact that it has given users the ability to access desktops. A remote desktop protocol serves as a bridge between desktops and users. While the novel concept itself resembles other computing models, what sets VDI apart is that it seamlessly strikes a balance between performance, security and manageability.

VDI is a solution, not a product, and as we take a look at the next sections, the reader will get a deeper understanding of desktop virtualization. Readers will not only be able to determine how they can use VDI as a guard against security threats, they will also be able to determine how this type of desktop management can influence the IT landscape for the better.

By coupling the benefits of server-based and distributed computing, desktop virtualization can offer

endless advantages, such as superior performance, simplified desktop manageability and improved stability.

In other words, desktop virtualization establishes itself as one of the strongest tools in an enterprise's arsenal to keep pace with the evolving and ever-changing technological landscape.

Virtual Desktop Infrastructure has claimed unprecedented popularity over the years, and for good reason. Mobile desktop solutions allow a user to manage and deploy virtual environments from a centralized location and permits safe transmission of files over a secure network infrastructure.

More and more organizations today are looking for ways to improve how desktops and applications are delivered. They have to balance their options while embracing new technologies, and VDI is successfully breathing life into all these ideas.

This establishes that in a bid to accomplish mobile workforce enablement, VDI has become one of most important IT trends. From remote workforce enablement to reduced costs, it is no wonder that VDI has gained popularity.

Want to find out how Virtual Desktop Infrastructure can work wonders for you or your enterprise? Read on!

CHAPTER 01

History of Desktop Virtualization- A Travel Back In Time

THEY say the past shapes the future. This is certainly true as far as Virtual Desktop Infrastructure is concerned. While the mere mention of VDI may bring to mind names of enterprises like VMware, what you do not know is that the idea dates back several decades and it is only now that we are able to see the technology coming full circle.

Desktop virtualization has deep roots in the past. Reshaping today's IT industry, the technology has armed IT professionals with the means to effortlessly consolidate their servers, increase efficiency and reduce costs.

Wondering how it all started? The history of desktop virtualization is fascinating, to say the least. By taking a look at it, you will get a good idea about how the technology served as bedrock for today's environment from a technical, as well as a business standpoint.

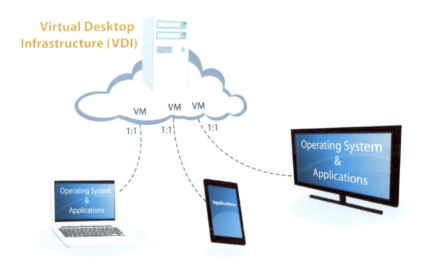

The Beginning

Desktop virtualization didn't rear its head on the IT landscape only recently. In fact, the idea came around four decades back during the 1960s. If you are wondering about the purpose the future-forward technology served around 40 years ago, you would be surprised to know that virtualization was introduced and employed to accomplish optimal hardware utilization.

IBM introduced virtualization in their environment around three decades back to serve the same purpose. The turning point in IT history came when IBM Cambridge Scientific Center set the wheels in motion for developing CP-40, an operating system that worked on the principles of a virtual machine time-sharing concept.

The technology was intended to address the spectrum of systems in the IBM environment that differentiated substantially from each other. New changes were being introduced, and each system had its own set of requirements. This made it exceedingly difficult for customers to use the systems to their advantage. Batch processing was the name of the game until now, but the existing systems were falling short of meeting the more advanced requirements.

First, IBM unveiled S/360, a mainframe system designed to serve a single user and would allow him to run batch jobs. However, with the emergence of ground-breaking computing concepts, companies like MIT and Bell Labs started seeking alternatives that allowed multiple users to simultaneously use computer hardware. IBM responded to this need with CP-40. As a main frame computer, it was never meant for the common public and was specifically designed for use in labs.

CP-40 evolved into CP-67. As the first commercially used mainframe supporting virtualization, it ran on an operating system known as CP/CMS. Here, CP is an abbreviation for Control Program, where CMS translates to

Console Monitor System. This operating system introduced user interaction into the equation for the very first time.

The approach used in the development of these systems was to simply divide system resources and memory among the users. The control program approach allowed every user to access a complete operating system. This idea simplified user operation significantly.

IBM played a pivotal role with the defining moment in history that allowed main frame computers to run several processes and applications simultaneously. By bringing virtualization into the picture, IBM facilitated users being able to make the most out of massive financial investments.

Virtualization on the backburner

During the eighties and nineties, computer technology progressed on the path to advancement by leaps and bounds. New ideas found their way into the limelight. The prevalent use of x86 servers, desktops and client-server applications introduced the plan for distributed computing. Windows was embraced for x86 systems and quickly claimed status as the industry's standard. However, with so much happening, virtualization was forced back to obscurity.

VMware breathed life into VDI

Virtualization of x86 systems was introduced in 1999 by VMware. It was a conscious effort to counter increases in infrastructure costs, ever-increasing demand of

desktop maintenance, disaster recovery, and last but not the least, desktop maintenance. VMware eliminates all these problems with adaptive virtualization where the virtual machines resemble each other in terms of hardware and successfully maintained software compatibility.

Application virtualization was also introduced, and since then, there was no turning back.

An In-Depth Dive in Desktop Management

Challenges have always been the part and parcel of desktop management. With the variety of execution models that are used, different management paradigms have strived to address these challenges. While each one of them has been successful to a certain extent with different success rates, it is crucial to take a look at all of these models.

Execution models

When computing, the relationship between the location of where the application is computed and the location of the interface device, has a direct influence on the manageability and performance of the user environment. This is because program execution can be clustered, distributed or centralized. Regardless of what an individual or enterprise opts for, there are always benefits and pitfalls associated with each one. Let's take a look at them.

- **Centralized Computing**

For many years, the complexity and expense of using centralized computing on early mainframe computers discouraged users and enterprises from making the most out of this scheme. Consumers were given the convenience to operate in stand-alone mode. However, they could only enjoy the flexibility by seeking support for different software running on their systems.

The emerging and ever-increasing consumer demands for affordable systems that operated on conventional operating systems such as Windows and DOS thrust the IT landscape into a realm where application software became a commodity rather than customer-centric creations of sound and skilled programmers. Enterprises quickly embraced PC technology, as this helped them easily access the software variety that was available for hardware at wallet-friendly prices.

- **Distributed Computing**

The idea behind distributed computing is to use a cluster of networked computers for an application in order to meet organizational needs. Till the start of mid-nineties, distributed computing accomplished phenomenal growth. While on one hand the PC became inevitable for the individual, on the other, enterprises reaped endless rewards because of the efficiency introduced in performance.

In the beginning when distributed computing was introduced, the network was simply an add-on, whereas it was the computing effort that served as the focal point. Networking was still in the cradle, and so design features like hard drives were introduced to fortify its growth. All these efforts were aimed at sustaining any personalization that had been introduced into a PC during reboots.

Distributed computing continued to be the prevalent computing model. All the performance and design assumptions introduced were centered on personal computers, since developers were under the assumption that a user would have exclusive access to a CPU and other resources. While desktop based software performed on servers as well, several standards adopted showed a tendency towards PC-centric designs.

- ## Windows Server-Based Computing

Ever since the large-scale deployment of PCs started, the IT management staff was forced to shoulder an ever-increasing burden of making frequent software updates. This made the task both tedious and prone to errors. When geographical dispersion was added into the equation, the situation worsened. Citrix then came forward with a new environment management approach in the mid-nineties.

This server based model introduced by Citrix retained the flexibility of the x86 Windows based software. What sweetened the deal were the centralized management and geographical consolidation opportunities this newly proposed approach created. Microsoft terminal server was quite similar to Citrix, as they both introduced session aggregation involving multiple users while using a single operating system.

The benefits this approach rolled out included easy upgrades, portability and competent user management.

These were factors that continued to make server-based computing one of the most widely used options in enterprises.

Before Virtual Desktop Infrastructure had emerged on the scene, it was only through terminal server and Citrix-based approaches that an enterprise could benefit from centralized computing. This was when the need for an approach like desktop virtualization emerged on the scene.

Demystifying Problems in Existing Server Design

The developments on Windows Kernel were designed with the intent of giving PCs the ability to effortlessly handle a wide variety of applications. The end-user has to be facilitated in addition to giving systems the ability to handle a wide variety of device drivers. This absolute focus on functionality came at a huge price tag. Crucial aspects of computing, like end-user isolation and multiple resource allocation, were forgotten, even though they were central to addressing multi-user workloads.

Sadly, a variety of issues reared their ugly heads when the Windows operating system embraced the multi-user functionality established by a terminal server. The issues that were introduced in Windows's general-purpose design are listed below.

- **Driver Incompatibility**

When performing under heavier workloads, devices and drivers started behaving in an unpredictable manner, and as a result, the probability of problem occurrence significantly increased. This lack of compatibility can be attributed to the fact that different vendors were not performing regression testing on device and drivers.

- **Performance Degradation**

With a focus on a PC-centric approach, the face of application designing changed in a way that consequently lead to performance volatility. Since operating systems were specifically designed to cater to user session densities, the unexpected workload negatively reflected on user experience. The biggest problem was when a CPU-intensive application was being used by several users on a server, and the other

users had to experience a significant performance degradation.

- ## Scheduling Limitations

Microsoft NT kernel introduced several innovations. However, even it failed to incorporate provisions concerning sophisticated resource allocations. The thread management that was introduced limited the ability of the computing model to balance workloads. If a time-consuming thread was executing, it could easily tie up 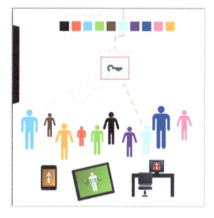 the processor's resources until the thread exited kernel and returned to user space. This establishes that one program had the ability to deny another one access to the CPU. This heavily degraded user experience under the workload of multiple users.

Terminal server-based computing grew tremendously in terms of popularity. Companies started acknowledging how valuable server based computing could prove to be. However, the compatibility and performance issues stayed the same and limited their capability. This was when desktop virtualization arrived and changed user desktop environments for the better.

CHAPTER 02

VDI- The New Face of Desktop Management

USING VMware's virtual infrastructure as the foundation, VDI can be described in layman terms as the practice of hosting a desktop OS within a virtual machine (VM). This virtual machine runs on a centralized server and is a variation of the server-based computing. Working on the principle of client-server approach, desktop virtualization was introduced as a means to address and resolve all those problems that terminal server based approaches failed to eliminate.

The ESX server introduced by VMware was designed such that it allowed several user desktops to run as individual machines while allowing them to share underlying hardware resources such as memory, networking, storage and CPU. This brought into picture the isolation of users from each other. Each user had an individual operating system. Most importantly, since the resources were allocated granularly, users did not have to put up with problems like application crashes. Users were also protected against problems in the OS that often used to occur because of other users.

Desktop virtualization explicitly cashed in on the features introduced by ESX server. Any inherent problems in server management were addressed as well. VDI was quickly embraced by enterprises on a large scale because it reduced the conventional issue of driver incompatibility. With virtual hardware, and by adhering to a hardware compatibility list, the ESX server seamlessly hosted hardware while keeping any problems or issues at bay.

The ESX server also addressed performance volatility by unveiling the CPU scheduling that supported scalability. Multi-host balance was introduced through Distributed Resource Scheduler (DRS). Another benefit introduced by the ESX server was that VMware made it possible to halt and reschedule a virtual machine regardless of the threads or activities being performed in the guest operating system. This resource sharing was more deterministic since it played a pivotal role in taking the user experience to new heights.

Unlike the terminal server-based computing model, VDI gave users independent VMs for better desktop computing. It is important to understand that running a terminal server, Citrix or any multi-user operating systems is not an example of Virtual Desktop Infrastructure. Instead, the ideas  behind desktop virtualization boil down to the fact that each user has his/her own operating system and that VDI offers them management features like performance and

stability, whichis imperative for the enterprise-wide adoption of the centralized computing model.

How Do Virtual Desktops Equate To Better Desktops?

For those who wonder how desktop virtualization penetrated so deeply and easily into the IT landscape, the answer is simple. VDI emerged as a secure, reliable, supportable infrastructure that improved user experience. The beauty of this revolutionary technology is that it is not tied to or managed by desktop machines heterogeneously. Regardless of operating system and end-user data, desktop virtualization allowed central management to IT staff. This made it significantly easier to enforce policies, protect data, and administer or upgrade desktop patches uniformly.

In other words, VDI satisfied the need for automation with several unique add-ons. With all the promises that were made to the customers, the technology addressed the shortcomings of existing computing models, and what served as a strong basis for the prevalent adoption of desktop virtualization was the significant improvements it secured in areas of security, manageability, costs and other areas. These benefits will be highlighted in the next section.

VDI for Enterprises- Transforming Corporate Desktop

ENTERPRISES opted for Virtual Desktop Infrastructure for reasons besides the inherent problems in the existing computing models. The factors that contributed to the large-scale adoption of technology were entirely different. A survey was conducted, and the improvements that were secured by VDI in different areas are depicted below.

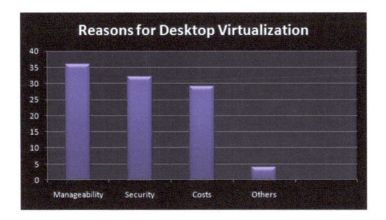

Let's understand each of these reasons for desktop virtualization in detail.

VDI- A Synonym for Management Made Easy

It is no secret that as far as enterprises are concerned, a large chunk of the total cost of managing desktop environment is consumed by operations issues, support and other user concerns.

Since VDI introduced the concept of centralized user environment where access was maintained through thin clients, the cost of operation observed a significant reduction. In desktop virtualization, each user has a centrally managed virtual desktop that mirrors his/her profile. This included upgrades for new software, and security, as well as those for existing software.

When standardization of such a high degree met centralized applications and data, the efficiency of the deployed system improved significantly. This established that clients were allowed to put entire user environments on autopilot. These environments would run anywhere and needed minimal management.

In terms of relocations, periodic replacements and rollouts, the clients earned an edge above personal computers because since no local storage is involved, no local installation is needed. Clients had a sustained service life and relocations could easily be handled by logistics staff.

VDI- Redefining Security

Security of data is one of the most prevalent client concerns. Since data is one of the most precious assets, it is crucial for clients to protect it. Studies have shown that misuse of information, data and internal information theft are some of the biggest problems to worry a company

owner. These are potential threats that enterprises have to deal with on a daily basis.

Enterprises intended to counter this problem through data backups where data and information from a company's resources were locally stored using CDs, DVDs and USB ports. However, this arrangement is not only costly, it was also known to have backfired in several instances. This made it even more important to opt for centralized data storage, and desktop virtualization emerged as an alternative to standard means of enforcing security provisions.

The benefit with desktop virtualization is that it transfers only graphical information to the designated terminal. Since it is only the contents of the screen that are being transmitted, the information is secured through encryption. The original data safely resides in the data center where backups are also maintained. This makes it significantly easier to protect the centralized server from malware and viruses. The concept is so simple that sometimes hackers don't even consider it worthwhile for preying.

Today, infrastructures cannot be protected against natural disasters such as a fire in a building. In the event of such a crisis, unlike a traditional approach, VDI makes it possible for employees to work from anywhere. While such disasters do restrict enterprises in business operation, VDI will allow them to at least maintain business.

Cost of Ownership- Biggest Benefit of VDI

When terminal services were introduced, they gained popularity as a cost-effective alternative to PCs. In the past, the cost savings that were introduced were offset by all those licenses that were needed. However, this is what earned desktop virtualization an edge over others because when coupled with open system architectures, VDI not only introduced savings but also eliminated dependency on software vendors.

Estimates showed that the savings increased up to 70% as compared to manually managed and administered workstations. Several aspects, such as boot time, employee productivity and electricity consumption have been aptly addressed by desktop virtualization.

Increased Flexibility

Workstations and desktop environments are bombarded with changes on an almost daily basis. This introduces a major cost and time factor that enterprises have to bear. Especially when new departments are launched, VDI clearly offers several benefits. These include quick configurations and availability of workstations in minimal time.

Since all the data and programs reside on servers, no configuration or installations are needed. Implementation and updates of software are also performed centrally and without any delay.

A Greener and Sustainable IT Environment

According to estimates, the IT industry produces around 600 million tons of carbon dioxide. This contributes to around 2 percent of emissions. To reverse this effect, a large scale plantation of 60 billion trees is needed. It is because of such statistics that the pressure on the IT industry is growing to take meaningful measures to eliminate this carbon foot print. This is when VDI steps in.

According to studies, when a personal computer is replaced by a client and terminal server arrangement, workstation emissions are reduced by a whopping 54%. It also results in low power-consumption, which translates into lesser noise and reduced amounts of heat produced.

This fortifies the production of fan-less devices, since VDI eliminates the use of processors for optimal performance and low power consumption, and in the new computing model, hard disk is removed. In several instances, these little changes have translated into higher staff productivity and well-being.

Another reason that enterprises opt for desktop virtualization is the service life span of clients. While traditional desktop computers come with a life of 36 months, the client-server VDI arrangements extends the life of the system up to 60 months. Listed above are the reasons enterprises are finding desktop virtualization as a remedy to several problems. It is this feasibility that has led

to the widespread adoption of VDI as a technology that can help businesses break free from babble and emerge on the landscape as a force to be reckoned with.

Benefits of Desktop Virtualization-Technology That Translates Into Endless Rewards

THE strongest feature of desktop virtualization is that the advantages which were once limited to distributed and centralized computing that have been combined by VDI. In this section, we will take a detailed look at what made VDI one of the strongest alternatives to conventional computing models.

First, let's take a look at the benefits VDI introduced in server-based computing.

VDI and Server-Based Computing Benefits

There is a set of benefits that is usually associated with terminal-server deployments. However, VDI rolls out the

same benefits. In fact, certain areas where server-based computing outshines the competition are also listed below as follows.

- VDI improves data security and integrity by restricting it within data centers. For instance, VDI saves administrators the inconvenience of updating desktops regularly with security patches. Instead of installing security patches on individual end-user desktops, the required patch simply has to be installed on the master image. After one reboot, all the VDI instances will be automatically patched.

- Upgrade cycles and consolidation is improved. In turn, this reduces hardware costs and the need for client-side equipment. The hardware for VDI may be expensive, but since the cost isn't recurring, the need for client-side equipment is significantly reduced.

- VDI makes management significantly easier with the centralized patching approach. Applications are installed and streamed without overloading the

network. This centralized patching not only saves time, but also it only takes minimum resources to accomplish the desired operations or tasks.

- The portability of user desktops is no secret. This makes it easier for users to connect to a variety of devices whenever and wherever they are. This flexibility has brought to life the idea of users accessing desired data and information in real time.

- The server-based computing model was always the preferred choice because of the way it pools resources. One of the most notable features of VDI is that it improves the ways in which resources are pooled and used to deliver optimal performance. Enterprises learned to put the server to work for them and instead of the resources being wasted in low-priority tasks, they are batched together so that maximum amount of jobs are performed using minimum resources in shorter time-spans.

VDI and distributed computing model benefits

If VDI offers benefits of server-based computing, it also retains some features that were previously associated with distributed computing solely. Since the distributed-computing model offers users access to their own operating system, VDI successfully retains all those features that distributed computing has to offer. Some of them are listed below.

- **User Isolation**

If observed closely, one acknowledges that in the case of terminal servers, user sessions govern the way applications perform. Sadly, sometimes a combination of software with complex workloads resulted in unexpected termination. This is when VDI emerges as a blessing in disguise.

The benefit of VDI is that it does not trust the stability of an OS to accommodate several users. Nor does it operate under the assumption that several permutations of software will work consistently and in a stabilized fashion. VDI simply protects users from any problems encountered by other users.

This eliminates OS crashes that affect several users simultaneously because VDI retains a certain degree of isolation that is often overlooked in the distributed computing models. This also gives users the ability to perform software installations and reboots without affecting anyone else on the server in the process.

- **Improved Performance**

When people use PCs, they assume they will have access to their own resources: memory, disk and CPU. This counters the problem of resource contention that servers usually suffer from. When heavy applications are introduced into the picture on a terminal server using published desktops, users may experience erratic performance because of performance degradation due to the existence of other users on the server. VDI completely eliminates such problems.

Things worked in favor of enterprises because they were able to deploy the centralized computing model

with the confidence that deployment of any new applications will be made possible without compromising user experience. This way, VDI borrowed the capacity of the distributed computing model while simultaneously maintaining the isolation of user environments.

Advantages for Desktop Management- Benefits That Know No Bounds

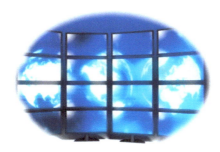

Desktop virtualization earned unprecedented popularity, and for good reason. It combined the flavors of terminal server-based computing and distributed computing, and introduced its own advantages, which are listed below.

- ## Stability And Performance Improvements

First and foremost, desktop virtualization is a computing model that allows users to consume resources located across a cluster of servers. User sessions are executed centrally without any dependence on the Windows kernel to coordinate sessions involving multiple users. This ability to create a group of users enjoying transparent migration between various hosts not only improves the type, but also the number of applications that can be seamlessly deployed on a server-based model.

- ## Reinventing Desktop Design

Through VDI, new bars were set for desktop performance, and the performance delivered by stand-alone PCs was easily challenged. This is accomplished through a different kind of memory management involving servers, gigabit networking and shared storage that breathed life into new and unique ideas for desktop redesign.

- **Maintenance Made Easy**

A benefit associated with VDI is that hardware maintenance can be carried out without any disruption. User sessions aren't interrupted, and there's no need for users to log off. What actually happens is that when the ESX server is in maintenance mode, any active VDI sessions are migrated to some other server in the cluster. This establishes that the IT staff can continue maintenance without disrupting the workflow.

- **A Unique Platform For Desktop Management**

When VDI was introduced, it was the very first time that enterprises got the opportunity to manage servers and user desktops. It not only simplified datacenter processes, but significant improvements were also accomplished between support groups and servers. It was now possible for a single design to be able to incorporate the disaster recovery to serve the needs of desktop and server areas.

- **Business Continuity**

Traditionally, users needed their own PC. However, VDI allowed them to take advantage of the portability that centralized computing brings into the picture.

Superior Performance Control Since VDI uses resource leveling for individual products, and this made it possible to control an application's priority within the servers. The idea of resource pools was brought to the limelight where user desktops were designated to different groups based on the priority they received on the network cluster. VDI also made it possible to execute applications that needed heavy CPU usage into separate pools across the cluster of servers.

- **Breaking Free From Several Computing Silos**

Terminal servers often had to shoulder the responsibility of segmenting applications between server pools because of application compatibility problems that reared their head. This called for each server to have a published group of applications where a certain level of fault tolerance is maintained,

regardless of how capable or incapable a server is. VDI introduced user isolation, which encouraged capacity-based server provisions. Eventually, this translated into a lower server count with a standard for countering fault tolerance.

- **New Opportunities for Application Management**

By using cloning and leveraging templates, IT administrators were given the authority to make machine templates and to deploy user desktops as the need arose. This is one of the biggest facilities VDI introduced for administrators. With VDI, they no longer needed to configure each desktop individually. Instead, by using templates and the features like cloning, administrators can earn the much-needed scalability of network as the need arises or as the number of end-users on the network increases. This not only helped save time, but any undesired inconvenience as well.

VDI made it possible for enterprises to allow employees to work remotely while keeping any potential security risks at bay. With virtualized desktops, employees were given the opportunity to access high-performance applications through GPU sharing, This GPU sharing is hardware-based and helps create a safe and secure connection to and from any device, even on low-bandwidth networks.

Desktop Stability- How It Works Wonders

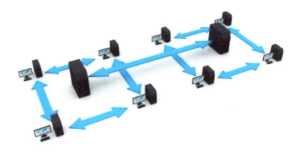

It cannot be denied that whenever an application is launched within an operating system, chances of conflict with other applications always exist. Sometimes, it simply leads to higher pressure on the underlying drivers, kernel scheduling and system services.

Desktop virtualization, in contrast, not only protects virtual desktops, it also protects them from any malfunction caused by the actions of any user. One had to acknowledge that there isn't a single multi-user platform in

existence that's free from hardware failures. However, what cannot be denied is that the hypervisor design used in the ESX servers offers a higher degree of protection to user sessions as compared to any shared services design that has been used in a terminal server.

Servers are managed such that when resources are managed through the kernel, a mini OS is built from scratch to ensure no problems are encountered in smooth resource allocation. The kernel is dependent on sophisticated and compact resource management, which made it possible for VDI desktops to share physical resources among themselves while successfully maintaining user isolation.

Chances of any faults at the kernel level are few as compared to all those system crashes that occur frequently with the use of Windows, and are now believed to be a part and parcel of it. This proves particularly useful for running a variety of heavy-load application software. The point is that since Windows has several services and functions running simultaneously, the chances of a conflict are higher than in the case of VDI's kernel.

The terminal server actually creates more chances for conflicts as compared to a single user personal computer. When rare incompatibilities arise, they manifest more frequently. This not only increases the number, but also the types of applications that are running simultaneously in the OS. This heightens the instability in the system that occurs as a consequence of the number of applications running at the same time. This happens because of the interaction between the applications and all that stress the OS bears.

In the case of a terminal server, if there are a total of twenty-five users and each user is running five applications simultaneously, the server will host 125 applications at the same time. The pressure exerted on the operating system is twenty-five times higher than an OS has to bear with a single user on the PC.

When this high pressure on the system is combined with the unbelievably high number of applications that are supported by the operating system, a high degree of instability inherently arises in the operating systems for all the users simultaneously.

In contrast, VDI offers each user an individual OS, and the risk of conflict occurrence is same as that experienced by the PC users with an individual OS. However, what sets VDI apart is that it mitigates those risks that a shared server host suffers from by allowing fatal conflict with one user to affect the other. This approach not only reduces the chances of conflicts that lead to large-scale disruption, but it also brings to light a computing model free from any chances of negative application interaction.

VDI and Cost-Effectiveness- How It Keeps Things Easy On the Pocket

VDI and cost is an issue that's widely debated. It is only when an enterprise takes into consideration the cost of ownership and other costs that the complete picture becomes clear. As understood, there are certain risks and costs involved in any management model or execution model. However, there are certain areas where desktop virtualization helps secure massive improvements, and these areas are outlined below.

- **Provisioning logistics:** When desktop virtualization is introduced, it leaves no doubt that deployment of infrastructure is significantly simplified.

- **Hardware maintenance:** Desktop virtualization reduces complexity that became a part and parcel of managing client devices in other similar arrangement. However, VDI eliminates this complexity since it not only utilizes the most advanced management options, it also guarantees that hardware maintenance is almost zero. This reduction in hardware maintenance is accomplished on the back-end through using thin clients or zero clients. If you opt for thin client hardware, the data center will be responsible for hosting the virtual desktops and the thin client will simply play its part as a terminal for the back-end server. This way, thin clients simplifies application access, improves security, brings ease of installation into the picture and reduces hardware needs. Hence, maintenance

is also reduced. Another alternative are the zero clients. Not only are they more cost-effective and slimmer as compared to thin clients, they don't necessitate any configuration and are tremendously useful when it comes to reducing hardware maintenance.

- **Hardware duration:** Desktop virtualization works on a model where resources are pooled and performance tuning and balancing is accomplished through it. This entails great flexibility that allowed the IT staff to host any combination of desktops virtually on the hardware. As performance needs arises, applications use hardware as it becomes available. This helps prolong the life of server hardware.

- **Less downtime:** When user-isolation is combined with server stability, the downtime that occurs as a result of software malfunctions is significantly reduced. Desktop virtualization has introduced several features that contribute to the reduced uptime for VDI setup. With features like high availability, desktops can restart automatically in the event of hardware failure. VDI has also introduced the ability for ESX servers to stay in maintenance mode. This allows desktops to migrate to other hosts without disrupting user sessions during Windows' maintenances. Since desktop virtualization is employed with a hardware compatibility list, the server still improves the uptime for VDI deployment.

- **System performance:** Areas of cost reduction that cannot be overlooked are the unique platform balancing, opportunities for optimal performance and resource allocation that eventually translates into better system performance.

- **Application management:** Due to the proximity within the datacenter, streaming applications are known to perform better in a desktop virtualization environment. Since the datacenter is located in the vicinity, it is easier to establish an Ethernet connection between supporting servers and virtual

desktops. Use of image strategies and templates of virtual machines also simplifies management.

Desktop virtualization rolls out countless cost-saving features and opportunities while successfully addressing the problem of user environments. The IT landscape will take some time in uncovering such opportunities, but the long-term cost-savings that desktop virtualization implies may allow enterprises to realize that the cost-effectiveness is closely tied to centralized computing.

In terms of software compatibility and stability, the server-based computing model has restricted these savings for enterprises who have not yet embraced the idea of centralized computing with arms wide open.

Thankfully, those who have employed desktop virtualization acknowledge that server-based computing should be their focal point and that they should work more aggressively to accomplish features like scalable performance, reduced application interaction and end-user isolation. It is only with this approach that successful deployment of future and current software can be made possible.

Pitfalls of Virtualization

Desktop virtualization is a great innovation in the technology world, to say the least. While on one side it cannot be praised enough, on the flip side, there are certain disadvantages that cannot be overlooked as well. The advantages certainly outweigh the  disadvantages, but there are certain aspects that must be taken care of in the production environment.

The disadvantages listed below are mainly those that an enterprise should take into account to have a clear picture of whether or not it is as promising a technology as it appears to be.

- **High Risk**

If a physical fault occurs, a high degree of risk is involved. The idea that five different servers virtually work within a single server is rewarding, but one aspect that people often overlook is the effect inflicted on the five servers if a single hardware failure occurs in the physical server. All five servers will go offline. It is a major pitfall associated with desktop virtualization that an enterprise should think about before deploying the computing model.

One may debate that this problem can easily be countered by having two physical servers with centralized storage and the same configuration to run them all in an environment. This way if one physical server fails, the five virtual servers can continue to operate smoothly without any negative impact. However, having more than one physical server will increase the cost and risk associated with centralized storage, more than one physical server and smooth server migration in this setup.

If we take the cost into consideration, it will be clear that the cost of getting a powerful server, network storage and installation will be the same as that of acquiring five physical servers that operate independently of each other. Similarly, if a single physical server hosts five virtual servers and the physical server catches fire or suffers from any other disaster, all five servers will go offline.

Thankfully, with backup storage, it will take us sometime to restore the hardware, but eventually the servers will start performing again.

- **Performance Issues**

If we have a virtual server with 4GB RAM and two virtual CPUs of 3GHz each to act as a web server in our office, will the server deliver a performance similar to running a physical server with 4GB RAM and two individual CPUs of 3GHz each? It is highly unlikely.

What we know is that the virtual environment doesn't support the applications and operating systems to talk to other hardware resources, unlike the way it

works with physical servers. This is also an important factor that enterprises should take into account while allocating and planning with virtual severs.

- **It's Not A Piece Of Cake**

As much as we may find it hard to believe, the truth is that managing or setting up a virtual environment for high performance servers in a production environment is not a piece of cake. Those who are experts in PC hardware will realize that management of physical servers is significantly easier, especially when all the configuration and hardware aspects are handled by Intel-based servers.

This is not so as far as desktop virtualization is concerned. Before deploying them, a user needs to accomplish a thorough understanding about technologies like hyper-v, Xen server or VMware to make it work. You need to invest time and energy to not only understand the idea, but also to make it work for you.

- ## Lack Of Compatibility And Support

There are certain applications that just don't support virtualization yet. Sometimes the application may face problems and behave in a virtual environment in an unexplained manner.

- ## Licensing Needs

Desktop virtualization is not something an enterprise can choose to embrace in one day. There are certain licensing needs that have to be met. From desktop virtualization licenses to network infrastructure, and from centralized storage to bandwidth support, desktop virtualization can only be adopted once all of these needs are met.

- ## No Reduction In Hardware

People are often under the assumption that they will be able to reduce physical hardware by deploying the VDI. This is something that just doesn't happen.

- **Purchase Costs**

Since a user will have to purchase licenses for applications and operating systems, there are no significant budget cuts that are secured here. In fact, sometimes VDI servers for thin client infrastructure are heavier on the pocket than expensive computers.

- **Need For Extra Bandwidth**

The network has to accommodate the need for any extra bandwidth that's introduced. If that's not possible, the infrastructure has to 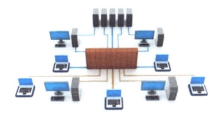 be upgraded. WAN links also need to have sufficient bandwidth to migrate users to other networks.

- **Compromised Quality**

If the bandwidth is not large enough to meet the needs or if the LAN suffers from congestion, the display quality rendered may suffer. It won't get anywhere close to the quality a viewer enjoys when images are

streamed from a server where applications are viewed and processed straight from the desktop.

- **Difficult Management Of HD Video**

HD video is not easy to handle when desktop virtualization is in question. To counter this problem, vendors often use methods that allow them to overcome this situation.

Despite all the pitfalls that exist, what cannot be denied is that desktop virtualization is one technology where the disadvantages pale in comparison to the advantages. The pitfalls may be many, but can easily be remedied, and there are always ways enterprises can turn-around these disadvantages to make the most out of the potential that this technology has to offer.

CHAPTER 05

Desktop Virtualization and Security

SINCE desktop virtualization has gained in popularity, the technology has come a long way. Enterprises are acknowledging the spectrum of benefits it has to offer. No wonder VDI is quickly becoming a strategic investment central to the IT infrastructure. Apart from its positive reflection in efficiency, productivity and flexibility, desktop virtualization has played a crucial role in desktop management by completely transforming the way businesses employ compliance and information security.

With advantages like flexible workplace, mobility, support for work styles and embracing diverse computing devices, the IT landscape is cruising along the lines of cost-effectiveness. Now, security had also joined this list of benefits. In fact, a vast majority of the enterprises that adopt desktop virtualization do so with the intent to secure improvements in the area of information security.

The security benefits VDI brings into the picture are inherent in the effective architecture that focuses on desktop, data and application centralization to eliminate those barriers that exist in delivery to devices.

This consolidation offers support for central management at a granular level. Policy-based control can also be exercised, and compliance requirements are supported through monitoring, reporting and the logging of information usage and access.

Flexible options for delivery of data, applications and desktops to authorized workers is introduced while

giving users the flexibility to use any type of end-point device they deem fit. From smartphones to tablets, from PC to laptops all the way to the thin client, an organization is given protection of information while making the most of user flexibility.

This leaves no doubt about why decisions of IT staff sway in the favor of VDI. Desktop virtualization is not only important for information protection, this aspect proves to also be highly effective and fast for providing access to desired information.

Implementation of VDI is in essence a security strategy that not only safeguards an organization's application and data resources, but also allows users to access them whenever and wherever they need them. This is a balance that can only be accomplished by introducing desktop virtualization into the equation. Organizations across the globe are of the same view, and that's why VDI has become a fundamental part of their security strategy. Keep reading to find out the pivotal role VDI plays for improving security.

How VDI Takes Security to the Next Level

Virtual enterprises are now the norm and with work styles and distributed workforces, there are new security challenges that are rearing their heads. In this scenario, VDI establishes itself as one of the most commendable strategies for controlling information resources and their accessibility.

Figures show that there are several organizations which are now adopting desktop virtualization. In most cases, the reason is to improve information security architecture. Security is one of the major concerns desktop virtualization addresses.

Research has shown that around 86% of IT staff who have championed the embrace of desktop virtualization in enterprises view it as a means to improve information security, regardless of the way it will be employed in the environment.

VDI- Where Security Meets Worker Flexibility

Effective management of environments is closely tied to improved security, and this relationship has

addressed many of the issues IT companies are currently facing. Many firms have fallen behind the trend of IT consumerization. Improved mobility, workforce flexibility and device proliferation are just added benefits one secures through desktop virtualization.

In today's world, data resides everywhere. From private and public clouds to enterprise networks, from worker-owned tablets to computing devices, and from smartphones to computers, one or another form of data exists everywhere.

The mobile workforce and the idea of a dispersed network now extends from customer settings to project sites, branches and site offices and in-between these locations. The larger part of the workforce employed in enterprises now wishes to break free from traditional employee models and is seeking alternatives that serve them better. Everyone falls under this umbrella, including outsourced vendors, agencies, temporary workers, contractors and consultants.

Desktop virtualization allows enterprises to not only maintain an environment based on distributed computing, but also makes it possible for them to seamlessly control their IT resources through  effective desktop, data and application management, while ensuring accessibility from several end-point devices.

This creates a secure infrastructure where risk management is addressed, and the need for device standardization in the computing environment is eliminated. Also, there is no need to enforce strict user policies, security measures or generic networks. In turn, all these factors contribute to help workers operate with flexibility in a user-friendly environment where productivity, customer service and business agility are greatly improved.

Research has shown that IT staff believes VDI to be incredibly effective in protecting information and providing workers unrestricted access to information they need and require.

Better Desktop Management Means Better Security

Desktop virtualization has not only enabled and improved desktop management, but has also brought into picture the ability to update and maintain individual personal computers. This has significant implications on information security.  Studies have shown that of all the security attacks attempted on a network, 90% are successful because of existing vulnerabilities that could have been easily safeguarded through secure configurations or patches.

The advantage of centralizing desktop, data and applications is that it is now significantly easier for the IT staff to deploy any security updates, patches or applications in a consistent and timely manner. This has trimmed down vulnerabilities to a great extent and several potential exploitations have been addressed as well.

This unique ability to instantly provide unrestricted access to information for any user, regardless of the location of his end-point, particularly serves as an invaluable feature for enterprises that rely on third parties to protect themselves against any posed threats, like employee malfeasance, for instance.

In other words, one can say that desktop virtualization is a chance for enterprises to aptly protect their information resources and guarantee compliance. Since the technology is complemented by several other security-based technologies, it creates safer and more secure infrastructures. Given all the benefits it has to offer, it leaves no doubt that VDI does serve as a doorway for information technology where security and safety knows no bounds.

CHAPTER 06

Desktop Transformation- Transitioning From Conventional IT Solutions

RECENTLY, there has been a lot of hype of about desktop transformation and what it has helped accomplish for the business landscape. So what exactly is desktop transformation, and what role has it played in transitioning enterprises, firms and companies from the most widely accepted solutions? The answer lies ahead.

Desktop transformation is all about using unconventional technologies like desktop virtualization to better deliver and manage desktops. Usually, when desktop virtualization is discussed, the question arises whether or not VDI is applicable for non-traditional desktops like iPads.

However, a more important aspect that is often ignored is the type of applications that works best with VDI and what the best strategy would be to adopt. Well, the answer is simple. First and foremost, application issues are a completely different topic from desktop transformation.

Applications are essentially solutions, since they are what users need to get any tasks done. When it comes to desktop transformation and application usage, there are options that exist on the hardware, as well as software side, for desktop transformation that must be taken into account. The different combinations will then be considered to determine which ones make the most sense based on the strategy you choose to use.

One aspect that needs to be addressed is that people often believe desktop virtualization goes hand-in-hand with application virtualization. Apparently, this is not one of the best options that exists. Instead, it is a better idea to deploy application natively in a virtual environment, especially when MSI-based applications are in question.

There is no point in believing that desktop virtualization is a solution where one size will fit all. In fact,

it has been found that static desktops, those with simpler configurations, lesser changes and fewer applications, are the best candidates for VDI.

The point we are trying to establish here is that when Virtual Desktop Infrastructure has to be implemented, application assessment should be performed to determine which applications are being used, how they are being used, what their infrastructure is, and which

requirements and aspects must be taken into account before one takes a dive. Once that is accomplished,

one can determine the right technologies for applications and desktops according to the statistics to find the right solution.

Desktop transformation can yield enormous benefits for both IT staff and users, provided it is done right. Doing so requires that all assumptions of one size fits all are avoided. Instead, one should plan thoroughly and assess options to determine the right technologies that

ensure all the requirements are effectively met. This is important because if a desktop cannot be transformed reliably and users don't feel the applications are performing in the desired manner, than desktop transformation is bound to fail.

Valuable Recommendations for Implementation of Desktop Transformation

It is no doubt that benefits of desktop transformation and modernization are enormous. Thanks to desktop transformation, IT firms have successfully reduced energy, money and time that was previously spent on user support and improving user experience by allowing users to access their workstation and application from anywhere and everywhere.

On the flip side, if desktop transformation is not employed wisely, it can lead to grave consequences like improved cost per desktop. The big question is, however, how does one keep all such problems at bay and ensure success? Our list of recommendations lies ahead. Go through them and cruise along the lines of success for desktop transformation.

- First and foremost, it is crucial to examine the inherent requirements of use cases. This involves finding out what the different tasks users perform will be, what the applications they use to accomplish them are, what kinds of access they need and how they plan work every day.

- Consider all the devices they will need to access. This not only includes PCs, mobiles and tablets. You also need to be well-versed about the devices your infrastructure will support and the relevant policies you need to enforce to accomplish it.

- Before making a decision, take security, networking and storage needs into account. What you can do is create non-functional teams that involve representatives from areas you have built around your strategy.

- Other aspects that go into decision-making are user experience and impact on your IT infrastructure.

- Understand that there's no point in treating desktops as servers. The characteristics and workloads they both support are entirely different. Instead, your focus should be on the characteristics of how your workforce performs their duties to address their needs in a more efficient manner.

- Evaluate different options, as this will help you determine which option will render the biggest savings.

- While there's no harm in considering different solutions, the problem arises when enterprises limit themselves to single virtualization vendors. You need to realize that in order to make the most out of this technology, it is a better option to leverage several users. Don't shy away from using a

combination of solutions, not only in terms of technologies, but in terms of vendors as well.

- The one size fits all theory doesn't apply in this case. That's why it is important to understand each individual use case to find the right vendor and right technology for each one.

The bottom-line is that employing VDI is not easy and there are several obstacles you are most likely to come across. However, if you start on the right foot, you can keep profits pouring in. Start by understanding your users, build a criteria, match variable technology to fit your needs, and once that is successfully accomplished, you can start evaluating vendor solutions for the ideal technology. User needs are changing and necessitate desktop transformation. On top of it, desktop transformation facilitates IT, and when planned carefully, desktop transformation through virtualization is the one turning point the landscape needs to create history.

CHAPTER 07

Comparing VDI Solutions- Evaluating the Options

IN the world of desktop virtualization, options for solutions are virtually countless. With the ever-increasing popularity of the technology, it is no wonder that new and more advanced technologies are rearing their heads on a daily basis.

While there are a plethora of options to choose from, the two solutions that cannot go unnoticed are XenDesktop by Citrix and VMware View by VMware. In this section, we will not only discuss them in detail, but will also take a look at other VDI vendors and their solutions. We will assess them and determine how they are different from each other and will briefly review their technical perspectives.

The first ones under scrutiny are XenDesktop by Citrix and VMware View by VMware. Before we launch into the  discussion about the feasibility of the two solutions, the first aspect that must be considered is that in the months to come, both VMware view and XenDesktop may adopt feature parity. However, for the time-being, enterprises are trying to make things work with the VMware's PCoIP. Sadly, this protocol is not just incompatible with the security server, history has shown that Citrix has maintained an edge over VMware for being a firewall friendly and client-friendly connectivity suite.

If narrowed down, there is one other disparity that becomes apparent. Citrix and VMware are both cost-effective when applied in a closed model where enterprises are required to deploy their solution, hypervisor and virtual desktop known as a broker.

There is no doubt that one point that works in the favor of XenDesktop is its compatibility with ESX. This makes it an ideal choice for enterprises that have lots of empty space on clusters. One wonders what happens when there isn't sufficient space capacity. What happens when hardware has been purchased for implementing a new VDI project and it is too big to be accommodated into the VMware's existing configuration? What if the structural and functional differences encourage the use of physical boxes running virtual machines and VMware and another machine running XenDesktop?

Why should one opt for such a configuration? The reason could be anything. You may simply feel uncomfortable with the block of servers running

simultaneously and the combination of workloads affecting production and virtual desktop. It is important to understand that instead of creating cluster of servers for individual tasks, the silo approach should be implemented, as it affects permission perspectives, performance, and management.

Apart from all the aspects listed above, the factors where the two solutions strive to outshine each other are listed below as follows.

Price

If asked, most people will tell you that VMware is expensive as compared to its counterpart. The story doesn't end there, though, because we know that when

VDI is implemented, the desktop is made capable of handling unique workloads. This makes virtual desktops significantly different from server consolidation, which was an idea introduced by both solutions in the previous decade. Virtual desktops are cost-effective, and perhaps it is this cost-effectiveness that virtual machines have protected the server.

If we look closely, we will realize that server commute has also been more expensive than desktop commute. A few years back, it was easier to create any proposition around consolidations. However, today, it is hard to accomplish with virtual desktops, especially in cases where the difference is not uncovered in the licensing models.

It is human tendency to try to accomplish more with as little as possible. When desktop virtualization was introduced, all the focus was on trying to do as much as possible with as little as we had.

With the two solutions that we possess, it can be easily seen that existing licensing models such as XenDesktop do not allow a blended solution with ESX.

Similarly, the combination of XenDesktop and VMware's view is also not supported. This will encourage users to perform apple-to-apple comparisons for projection involving virtual desktops, which is one aspect they unwittingly ignored when working on projects involving server consolidation.

The Hypervisor

Another difference is the idea of 'just enough hypervisor' that has started gaining popularity in enterprises that aim to implement it. These proposed hypervisors are essentially virtual machine monitors. As a piece of hardware, software or firmware, hypervisors are responsible for running and creating virtual machines.

Now more and more virtual desktop solutions are built around a just-enough hypervisor approach. For several years, vendors created specific stock, keeping units for blended solutions. This was expensive, and sometimes the solutions were over-featured for the tasks that had to be accomplished.

What enterprises needed was a hypervisor with enough features, one where any unnecessary features should be eliminated. XenDesktop attempted to take this approach and successfully implemented it.

On top of that, this is a sound strategy to find out how well one vendor performs against another. Simply put, if you create a virtualization platform using a single vendor, it becomes difficult to convince contacts that you seriously wish to assess the competition.

Going down the multi-vendor route may be expensive and complicated, but since most of the vendors already work in a multi-vendor environment, this is not a problem thatwill raise eyebrows. The beauty is that it also helps secure significant sums of money if seen from a licensing perspective. The money saved can then be used for hardware improvements or staff trainings.

On a final note, one can say that while Citrix's XenDesktop is a decent choice as far as VDI is concerned, not the hypervisor. XenDesktop is competing with VMware's view as both are some of the most widely used VDI solutions. However, users are of the opinion that

XenDesktop is the better out of the two VDI solutions. XenServer and ESXi are decent choices for hypervisors.ESXi and Microsoft were competing against Citrix XenServer. However, Citrix is consistently making efforts to improve its hypervisor and these attempts can certainly serve as a foundation Citrix needs to establish its foothold in the data center. This is half the battle won because only smaller leaps are needed now to run not only virtual desktops on XenServer, but also on server-based virtual machines as well.

Other Noteworthy Solutions

We will now take a look at all those solutions that successfully outshined others and played in the big leagues. The brief description of each VDI solutions is intended to help you develop a better understanding of all those options that are available in the VDI space.

- **Ericom Power TermWeb Connect**

Ericom is a name that needs no introduction. With a legacy of offering industries and organizations access to data, desktops and applications running on Microsoft terminal services, Ericom is known for its superior VDI services, cloud platforms, end user computers and mobile devices.

The VDI solution Ericom unveiled was Power TermWeb Connect. As a comprehensive and unique access solution, the highlights of the Power TermWeb Connect are the ability to access and manage applications, cloud platforms, desktop and data centrally. This solution is not only cost effective, but gave organizations the ability to establish a connection that is secure and easy to operate. The solution is fast and promises a superior user experience over slow or low bandwidth connection.

On top of it, Ericom uses a scalable SSL gateway and offers support for three access protocols namely Microsoft RDP/RemoteFX, AccessNow and RDP accelerated by Blaze. Every single edition of Ericom incorporates Ericom blaze (for compression and acceleration of RDP), Ericom AccessNow (as an RDP solution for HTML5), Ericom AccessToGo (RDP client

native for Chrome, Android and iOS) and last but not the least, Ericom secure gateway (SSL).

- **Citrix VDI-in-a-box**

Several customers were not embracing VDI because of the high deployment cost and complexity desktop virtualization ensued. Citrix addressed it with its unconventional launch, VDI-in-a-box. With affordability on the one hand and ease of use on the other, this solution enabled administrators to centrally manage desktops for any user, anytime and anywhere, and at a cost that can easily rival the other solutions in question.

This solution eliminated complexity almost effortlessly through connection brokering, desktop provisioning, load balancing and availability of virtual appliance. The infrastructure was significantly improved as well while the need of shared and management servers was eliminated. VDI-in-a-box, also known as Kaviza, gained further popularity by providing support for latest versions of VMware vSphere, Microsoft Hyper-V and Citrix XenServer.

The nucleus of the system was VDI Manager which performed functions like creation of virtual desktops by means of an existing template. This solution manages load by balancing it across the grid. Servers are enabled to communicate proactively so as to make it easier for servers to share configuration and operational information back and forth.

This solution implements a user-friendly interface. It comes with two licensing options: perpetual and annual where a customer acquires the license by paying for it only once and can use it on a perpetual basis as a need arises. In the other case, the license can be acquired for 12 months and it is mandatory to renew the license if the customer wishes to keep using the solution.

- **Dell vWorkspace**

Dell's vWorkspace, formerly known as Quest, was essentially the result of Provision Networks' acquisition by Dell. Provision Networks was a company that intended to eliminate all of the barriers that stood in the path of virtual desktop application delivery and deployment.

Quest vWorkspace promises to deliver desktop and virtual applications using multiple hypervisors, blade PCs and desktop services. The focal point of this solution is Experience Optimized Protocol. Abbreviated as EOP, it embraces and extends Microsoft's RDP protocol to deliver a superior user experience.

vWorkspace uses a connection broker and other important parts incorporated into this solution are vWorkspace interface, SSL gateway and database. This solution has three license types: enterprise, desktop edition and premier.

- **Desktone**

Desktone was originally developed to address the need for a desktop service that can be hosted on clouds. In 2008, desktop launched a platform for virtual desktops. In other words, Desktone introduced the novel concept of using cloud-hosted desktop as a Service. Several industry giants such as IBM partnered with Desktone to encourage users to embrace desktop as a service.

As far as functionality is concerned, Desktone took ease to new heights. All a customer has to do is to submit a web form for creating a tenant and a series of actions are triggered like creation of VLAN, provision of management appliances and connection broker on the VLAN and a storage point for desktops.

This solution eliminates operational complexity and brings ease of use and simplicity into the picture. Virtual appliances that are Linux-based bundle three software modules like desktop manager, access manager and resource manager. Apart from the facilities these software modules provide, what makes Desktone truly unique is that it has been designed to deliver DaaS from the ground up.

Desktone introduced a platform that was not only scalable but kept things easy on the pocket as well. The beauty of Desktone is that it supports the highest number of desktop virtualization technologies such as dedicated windows server desktops, remote desktop services and dedicated virtual desktops hosted on servers.

- **LISTEQ BoXedVDI**

LISTEQ made its mark in the desktop virtualization space with BoXedVDI. As a unique "plug and play" alternative, it helped organizations break free from the conventional VDI solutions. Unlike traditional solutions that were focused on server side, BoXedVDI was not only easy to deploy, it made it possible to manage VDI solutions that incorporated hardware, OS agnostic and hardware.

In addition to support, BoXedVDI offers access to native protocols over USBs. It uses Oracle Virtual box as a native hypervisor and since it runs on the hypervisor's native layer, it supports any and every OS running within hypervisor. BoXedVDI uses an interconnectivity protocol that simplified management for users. BoXedVDI uses native storage for different hypervisors and enables customers to use cost-effective NAS and SAN solutions. As far as licensing matters, it can be acquired on perpetual basis or a monthly subscription can be obtained as well.

- **NICE DCV**

NICE is actually a consulting Services company dedicated to reducing hardware costs and improving productivity. The solution it introduced in the market Desktop Cloud Visualization or DCV for short. Accomplishing the perfect balance between high-performance computing and ease of work management, NICE uses an HPC portal offering.

This portal is committed to providing access to data, interactive application, data, HPC clusters, infrastructures and so on. Whether it is parallel job submission or computation intensive tasks, this portal introduced by NICE allowed users to discover, explore and create in a more efficient manner.

DCV actually consists of three components: self-service portal, abstraction layer and resource control and computational and storage resources. The self-service portal allows scientists and engineers to access data and applications in a web-based setting. This makes it easier to maintain the integrity of data without any need individual software installation. The

abstraction layer and resource control, on the other hand, are responsible for remote virtualization, interactive workloads, and resource provisioning and data management while ensuring a superior user experience. Here it is worth mentioning that this layer is not visible to end-users, as it lies underneath the portal.

The computational and storage resources maintain any newly provisioned or existing resources of the organization such as memory, servers, HPC schedulers, visualization servers, GPUs as well as the storage to host models, application binaries and intermediate results.

This solution is quickly gaining popularity with the customers as enterprises now have the flexibility to create and secure that engineering clouds without the need for any massive network upgrades. Since this solution also safeguards data, there is no need to transfer or stage data on a workstation. In other words, BoXedVDI is dynamic, scalable, powerful and simple and these are certainly qualities that any enterprise would enjoy.

Understanding VDI - What Sets It Apart

MANY companies have resorted to desktop virtualization, and with all the benefits the technology entails, it is no wonder that implementation has been significantly simplified and operating costs have been trimmed down phenomenally. On top of it, it is ensured that robustness of the infrastructure is maintained against natural disasters.

Most of the administrators who deploy virtual desktops prefer to host them in the data center. In the recent years, more and more people have embraced cloud technology, and in this section we will determine whether or not the possibility of hosting a desktop on clouds exists

and if it is a sound option to add to your list of business goals and objectives.

The Emergence of Desktop as a Service

Desktop hosting on clouds is possible. Abbreviated as DaaS, it is an approach that has allowed the IT world to easily outsource virtual desktops to your cloud service provider. A lot of times we assume that Virtual Desktop Infrastructure and DaaS are different from each other. What we don't know is that these services both share similar benefits, like reduced hardware, increased flexibility, improved mobility, simplified desktop management and a lot more. However, DaaS has its own set of challenges, such as data control, licensing and security.

Understanding Desktop as a Service

Want to find out why the idea of DaaS is quickly striking a chord with enterprises? The answer lies below.

- By introducing DaaS into the picture, the IT staff will no longer be responsible for maintaining the infrastructure. The difference between DaaS and

VDI is that the desktops hosted on clouds are least bothered about the technology that runs in the background. In simpler words, resource provisioning, network issues and load balancing are problems only the provider is concerned with. However, IT staff still needs to manage virtual applications, clients and desktops, and pay attention to remote desktops.

- Cloud-based services are a bigger attraction for enterprises because it not only reduces infrastructure costs that are inherent to VDI, but also because they make more sense for organizations that specifically rely on web-based apps. Still, IT staff prefers desktop virtualization because of data security, centralized management and optimal performance that VDI helps deliver.

- Cloud-hosted desktops help secure significant cut-downs on costs. Complexity is reduced as well. If you don't want to be concerned with back-end or end-points, DaaS may be a better choice. For an enterprise that lacks in-house VDI expertise, DaaS is

a better choice. An advantage of cloud-hosted desktops is that there are no PC costs involved. They are also known to operate faster and more smoothly because they aren't behind a firewall. However, since these desktops use a remote connection, some latency does exist.

The Ideal Choice: VDI or DaaS?

Understand that when cloud-hosted desktops are implemented, they are not connected to any servers that reside in the data center. This makes it easier to patch, move, upgrade or restore in the event of a failure. Cloud desktops are more flexible, and it is hassle-free to transfer a desktop to users on any desired device. This is a chance for companies to completely eliminate network concerns because cloud-desktops are connected to the environment through private connections.VDI, undoubtedly, trumps DaaS as explained in the following section.

How VDI outshines DaaS

Despite all the benefits listed above, it cannot be denied that VDI is a technology much superior to DaaS.

Read on to find out how and why VDI emerges as a clear winner for all your needs.

- While there are those who champion cloud desktops, there are reasons why one should be wary of them. Trust, for instance, is a major challenge facing enterprises. Enterprises should opt for VDI because the IT staff fails to exercise the same control they have over data in a VDI environment. Reliability and connectivity are other issues that haunt those who deploy cloud desktops. In other words, a provider has to devise other ways of keeping data secure.

- Another problem is the licensing issue with DaaS. In several environments, the service provider offers a document called SLA. The organization still needs to purchase a Windows license for each user. Since Microsoft doesn't have a license to offer so far for Windows 7, this makes it especially difficult for companies and firms to implement cloud desktops at low costs.

- Another problem is that while you have limited options to choose from for providers for VDI, when DaaS is in quickly, enterprises only have a few options. They also have to think of ways to deal with any unpredictable problems or issues that arise. Initially, an enterprise may be happy to deal with such petty issues but in the long run, they become troublesome. These problems that enterprises have to take care of are listed below as follows.

  - ✓ Finding out whether or not the service provider will offer any compensation if power outage occurs.

  - ✓ Ensuring that no compatibility issues rise.

  - ✓ Finding out whether or not USB support is offered.

  - ✓ Determining where the user profiles will be stored.

  - ✓ If any profiles exist that cannot be customized.

- DaaS suffers from other inherent difficulties as well. The user environment cannot be personalized. On the other hand, with VDI, admins have the power to customize desktops and personalize end-points to a certain extent. Another consideration that cannot be ignored is that both cloud desktops and VDI have desktops where there's a competition to use resources. To counter this, ensure that the system is well-equipped to deal with the extra load.

- If a cloud service provider will be handling your data, determine who will own it and then make a decision about how you plan to manage it. At the same time, you have to make sure the DaaS provider complies with technical and licensing regulations.

A Sneak Peek at Desktop Types: Persistent vs. Nonpersistent VDI

Having understood how VDI stays on top of organizational needs and maintains its effectiveness above other tools and technologies, we will now take a look at how different desktop types can be used to meet diverse requirements.

When employing Virtual Desktop Infrastructure (VDI), enterprises have two options to choose from: persistent and non-persistent. This final section of the eBook will shed light on it to help you make the most out of the choices you make.

With persistent desktop, each user gets his/her desktop. Non-persistent desktops, on the other hand, work on the many-to-one approach, which implies that a single desktop will be shared among several users simultaneously. Each setup has its own pros and cons and we will now take a sneak peek at how each arrangement works.

Persistent VDI

Also called one-on-one ratio, an individual disk image is used to run a desktop. Each user's settings are protected and appear on their own at the time of login. The benefit of this type of desktop is that it permits more personalization. A pitfall is that they need more backup and storage space as compared to non-persistent desktops.

The benefit is the ability to personalize and the superior degree of customization that can be accomplished. Individuals can easily access their shortcuts, files and data from the same desktop at every login. This feature encourages users to opt for VDI easily. In addition, persistent VDI has, more or less, the same setup as the one used in physical desktops. This not only simplifies management, but admins are saved the inconvenience of reengineering desktops as well.

Storage is a major concern for those using persistent VDI. Since disk images are required for each individual, more storage capacity is needed. Persistent VDI stores data on separate drives. These drives are then integrated with

underlying VMs, whereas the desktop is stored on the desktop. Quite recently, more features and storage products have been introduced for persistent VDIs to eliminate some constraints. Still, it cannot be denied that it was this storage concern that kept administrators from embracing VDI in the past.

Non-persistent VDI

Unlike persistent VDI, when users log out, their data and settings aren't saved. When the session ends, the desktop returns to its initial image and the user gets a new image every time he logs in.

The benefit of non-persistent VDI is that since they are made from master images, it's significantly easier for admins to update or patch the image, deploy it to users or back it up. Users, however, cannot make alterations or install apps. This makes the image secure. Also, if an image is compromised or hacked, the desktops can be rebooted to a clean state.

This means that there are no storage issues that an individual has to deal with. Since the user needs to configure data and settings separately and they are stored on individual hardware, they can easily be accessed remotely. This separates user data from the operating system and allows users to store data on low cost drives.

However, the pitfall of non-persistent VDI is that personalization is not permitted and application flexibility is compromised. This happens because non-persistent VDI doesn't use individual user profiles. The reason they are sometimes preferred by organizations is because the staff doesn't want to deal with profile management. The user profiles can be configured to allow users to delete themselves.

Since all the users are sharing one master disk image, customization will be needed to allow users to access all the apps they need. To implement it, environment virtualization or application virtualization is needed, which actually gets complicated. Another problem is that not every application can be virtualized, which limits the options in terms of the applications that can be used.

Each organization has different needs. Both options can prove to be useful, provided you have a clear idea of

the needs that have to be addressed. Depending upon the requirements, any enterprise can turnaround VDI solutions to make the most out of them.

VDI and IOPS

Storage planning is undoubtedly one of the most complex, yet crucial aspects of implementing any VDI solution. One mistake commonly committed at this point is that most enterprises take the same conventional approach to storage design that they have always practiced with server environments. Vendors assumed that a few lab tests would reveal to them the IOPS requirement and they could easily iron out any wrinkles that stood between them and appropriate implementation of VDI solutions. However, this is not what happens.

Once enterprises start using VDI solutions, it becomes apparent that storage requirements for VDI are a different story altogether. This is because while server-based infrastructures are constant in terms of load, this is certainly not the case with VDI environments. There may be some exceptions, but generally VDI environments are unpredictable as far as storage needs are in question.

This is also because those who prefer server-based infrastructures do so because of storage constraints whereas those who choose VDI environments do so with the intention of improving performance. This does not suggest that server-based environments do not take storage considerations into account. However, it cannot be denied that the reason they are preferred is their steady storage requirements.

Today, disks are becoming bigger and better whereas the IOPS on each disk stay the same. This makes it inevitable for any enterprise to unravel the mystery surrounding the GB/IO ratio. Lab tests show the Read Write ratio for VDI environments as 70-30%. However, in the real world, it is most likely 15-85%. Since majority of storage infrastructures are space centric, they are addressed with RAID 5 volumes.

This establishes that if a VDI environment is read intensive, the amount of IOPS required will be lower in volume than needed. This means that in order to deliver the amount of IOPS needed, more disks are needed, which will definitely strain the budget further.

The problem is, even after accurate calculation of spindles and the amount of IOPS that are needed is performed, aspects like latency, block size and read write ratio introduce new bottlenecks. Here it cannot be forgotten that different VDI solutions handle workloads differently and it goes without saying that all storage is not created equal. Similarly, not all VDI deployment models are the same. Each deployment model has its set of strength and weaknesses and the sizing considerations vary accordingly.

So, how do enterprises manage this need for IOPS? What is the most viable way to plan them? How solid-state drives fit into the VDI architecture? Answers to all these questions are outlined below.

The question is: when a vendor plans to implement a VDI solution, how many IOPS should be planned for each desktop? In case of traditional laptops, getting a cheap magnetic disk which has around 50 to 80 IOPS is enough. Those selling the software may suggest that 7 to 10 IOPS are sufficient.

This is because IOPS are expensive and the less you have, the less the VDI solution will cost you. This helps vendors sell more products. They are of the opinion that a user won't need more than 10 IOPS on an average each day. These assumptions might be true and for an individual who's accustomed to using around 50 IOPS each day, not only the performance degrades, a huge lag is created.

Another aspect that often goes unnoticed is that it may happen that a user loads an application. He may be maxing out all the 50 IOPS that exist. For the next one hour, they don't use any of the IOPS and then they save something and spike an IOPS appears on the usage graph again. Now, if the same user only has 10 IOPS to use, it will obviously take much longer to perform the smallest of operations.

What's the solution? The use of solid storage devices or SSDs. SSDs should be preferred over magnetic disks for several reasons: first and foremost, SSDs accommodate more IOPS than disks. Secondly, if an enterprise is well-aware that the maximum IOPS a user

might need are 50, there is no point in using the 10 IOPS per user baseline as a reference.

This means that before deploying a VDI solution, an enterprise should be well aware of its users' needs. Go for the highest possible number of IOPS and while it varies from scenario to scenario, an enterprise can use different alternatives to determine what best suits their needs.

Another question that arises is how administrators can employ solid state most effectively. Here it is important to understand that solid-state is a word that translates into different things for different users. For some it's dynamic RAM, while for others, the term boils down to caching. Since it is not affordable for an enterprise to have hundreds of IOPS for each of its users, some efficiency has to be introduced.

For instance, if several virtual machines are using the same block of data, provisions can be made to consolidate all the data into a single block. Another aspect that enterprises ignore is that each user may have their own set of data, but there's certain data that's the same between users such as the OS version, registries and kernel.

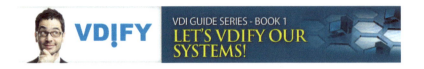

In other words, there are several blocks of data between users that are same.

Now, if there's a block of data that all the users or several users will be using and is shared among all the virtual machines, this block can then reside in a cache. It can either be accommodated on a high-performing area of cache or it can reside on an SSD or DRAM. Now if this block is served by memory, then we have thousands or maybe millions of IOPS because it is all memory.

The most effective way to use your storage space in a VDI environment is to plan it intelligently so that blocks of similar data can be consolidated and shared among all users. Even if we have several users, with 20 GB drives each, if around 2GB of it can be cached then we will have the maximum number of IOPS and it will be possible for us to use storage space in a VDI environment intelligently.

The Final Word- The Way Forward For Businesses

AS we come to the end of this eBook, we can derive the conclusion that when desktop virtualization is one of those technologies which, when coupled with complementary products, retains the best features of distributed PCs as well as server-based desktops. Opening up new management and performance possibilities, it can be a priceless adoption to a company's existing infrastructure.

Wireless technologies are dominating the landscape, and with their prevalent usage, there is little to no need left for working offline. This is where the adoption of VDI can become particularly useful, because by improving memory and CPU designs, the benefits of centralized computing can be elevated to new heights while improving the way resources are used and shared.

VDI successfully positions itself as a strong rival of the server-based computing model with the unique security and performance characteristics it adds into the equation.

To say the least, desktop management is evolving, and VDI is at the heart of it. Using a combination of distributing and terminal server computing, VDI has opened up a landscape where chances of using shared resources in the best manner are ripe.

With the wealth of wisdom revealed in this eBook, it leaves no doubts that applications which don't need to use CPUs heavily can leverage terminal servers. At the same time, published desktops and heavy applications can transition towards VDI to cash in on opportunities like resource allocation and isolation to improve user experience at every single step.

In fact, with the rate VDI is being embraced, it won't be wrong to say that VDI can actually eclipse all the other technologies in the years to come and claim a dominant position in the IT landscape. So, do you want your enterprise to secure its ease of operation, simplified management and other benefits? If yes, adopt desktop virtualization and cruise along the lines of simplicity and flexibility that you never knew existed.

Author's Bio

KHALID ALSHAFIE is a gifted IT professional with thirteen years of experience in successfully deploying large-scale desktop virtualization and cloud-based projects, as well as lots of experience with Data Center systems planning, designing, deploying and operations. He is currently serving as the Lead System Engineer in Citrix Systems and since 2011, he has led and executed IT projects for multinational corporations such as Volvo, IBM and Unisys.

With a long list of accomplishments to boast of, Khalid plans to help enterprises operate smoothly through desktop virtualization. He intends to play a pivotal role in reshaping the IT space while ensuring that client needs are met.

This Book is the first in his line of a VDI guide series, and with the wealth of wisdom revealed in this Book, he plans to help enterprises acknowledge new and exciting

reasons for embracing desktop virtualization as one of the most viable options.

Khalid Alshafie is associated with the Microsoft Tech-Ed IT forum and participated as a subject-matter-expert in the Microsoft IT Forum in Denmark and Microsoft TechEd in Netherlands. He has been nominated for Microsoft's most valuable professional (MVP) as well. For more information visit his web site **www.vdify.com** and follow him on Twitter **@vdify**

www.ingramcontent.com/pod-product-compliance
Lightning Source LLC
Chambersburg PA
CBHW041142050326
40689CB00001B/457